A FATHER'S LOVE

A FATHER'S LOVE

Asaph Brown

ISBN: 978-1-6653-0788-8 - Paperback
eISBN: 978-1-6653-0789-5 - eBook

These ISBNs are the property of BookLogix for the express purpose of sales and distribution of this title. The content of this book is the property of the copyright holder only. BookLogix does not hold any ownership of the content of this book and is not liable in any way for the materials contained within. The views and opinions expressed in this book are the property of the Author/Copyright holder, and do not necessarily reflect those of BookLogix.

⊗This paper meets the requirements of ANSI/NISO Z39.48-1992 (Permanence of Paper)

013024

I would like to dedicate this book to those individuals who are in the fight to be a part of their child(ren)'s life. Know that you are not alone. There is help there and it may be an uphill battle, but with God on your side, nothing's impossible!

CONTENTS

TO YOU, MY DAUGHTER

Dear daughter, you may not be able to read this for a while, but I wanted to apologize for the time that I missed during your first years on this earth. I missed seeing your first steps. I missed the times that you cried for me; I didn't get to be there to celebrate your birthday. I want you to know that I will always love your mom for bringing you into this world and being your mother. You are the reason I became a better man and continue to strive to be a better person every day. I always planned with you and your stepmother in mind. Always remember that family is everything. Don't live with hate in your heart. "Honor your father and your mother so that your days may be long on the earth" (Exodus 20:12) I may not always be around, but I will be here for you when you need me. Be strong my little butterfly.

Love, Dad

CHAPTER 1
GENESIS: HOW IT BEGAN

Marriage can be tricky! And, no, I don't want people coming to me saying it's the best thing that can ever happen to you. I mean, it indeed is, but it comes with its own set of challenges. We often romanticize it as a beautiful experience anyone can ever go through, but that allows people to turn a blind eye to the ugly side of it. Marriage can be delightful if both partners are committed to one another. However, being committed to this idea forever should mentally drain someone. Learning what to expect from your partner means meeting all your needs and accepting the potential for something outrageous.

Having high expectations can uplift your standards. Nothing is wrong with wanting love, commitment, honesty, and trust, but believing in never disagreeing can leave you in the dumps. Having realistic expectations of your life as a couple will leave you with a more robust future bond.

But that is what all people say, it's something you will find in the scriptures or your favorite romance novel. From my experience, even if you invest your soul, compassion, and comfort and show unconditional love to someone, you may still lose your loved one. It's possible, but there is no guarantee of your future.

Regardless of how much you contemplate relationships before you tie the knot, the months when you start planning your vows may throw you off. Putting the pressure of your entire emotional, physical, and financial well-being on your partner can be extremely draining. Consulting with one another before you make this decision or through your tough times is necessary.

Your insecurities aren't going to change after you get married. You will remain the same; therefore, building expectations from your partner might be useless. No marriage is perfect; learning how to compromise on other shortcomings is something you know along the way.

I wish to educate my readers on the bumps and bruises they might face in their marriage. I also want my readers to invest their time in family planning to provide their kids with a bright future and a sound upbringing. Ideally, you must sort out your finances when considering having a baby. The idea is to build a foolproof financial plan that provides a ladder for your child's growing needs.

When you bring a child into this world, it's utterly dependent on you. Educate yourself on a suitable insurance policy and opt for a term plan with at least ten to fifteen times your monthly income. This tends to increase security for their future in case something unforeseen happens.

Not only this, but after reading my book, I want my audience to familiarize themselves with all the legal rules about child custody and divorce. For instance, in my case, unfortunately, I had no clue how to fight for myself in court. I have been wrongly accused, blamed, and targeted for acts I never committed, and now I am under severe financial stress. I must provide for my daughter when I can barely make ends meet. Therefore, through this traumatic experience, I wish to spread awareness which could help my readers to be prepared if ever faced with issues relating to child custody.

Curating a plan before bringing a life into this world is paramount. A child has both short-term and long-term needs. Their long-term conditions, such as higher education, marriage, or mutual funds, must be brought into their consideration. Avoid traditional insurance plans as they aren't effective and fail to beat inflation—all the returns on the endowment and money-back plan range between 4 percent and 6 percent. Always include your child in every insurance plan you ought to take. After investing in life insurance, dive deep into medical insurance coverage. While at it, don't forget to keep the short-term goals in mind. Mentally prepare yourself for tuition fees, school fees, and other activities.

You might initially feel intimidated, but I intend to allow my readers to gain a realistic perspective of marriage as I navigate through my suppressed emotions sharing my story. Love isn't enough for marriage; you need to establish solid foundations. Besides building a deep level of trust, you must be honest with your partner. Discuss bills and divide responsibilities before tying the knot or moving in with someone if you aren't seeking marriage with them.

Sometimes, we all seek love that was lost somewhere, the love we thought we deserved but never received. I was also searching for this kind of love, but I had no idea I would be so unfortunate. It all started when I was around ten years old. I had developed a strong sense of how my emotional needs were met at this time. I could feel hatred, anger, love, stress, and sadness. I had grown enough to distinguish between them, not just me. All kids my age could name the emotions they felt back then.

The safest form of love I felt was from my dad, hero, mentor, and everything. I used to call him by my favorite superhero, Batman. I would eagerly wait for him to return from work so we could play a quick game of hide and seek. He would always shout out, "Fee Fi Fo Fum, I smell two little boys in this room," before he would come and find us. We would then have dinner together, brush our teeth, and get tucked into bed. However, this beautiful relationship I had with him was short-lived.

Our bond, fostered with respect, honesty, and trust, was soon twisted into something unknown. It all happened when my father separated from my mother due to personal differences. I was devastated when this happened. When my father separated from my mother, I was shaken. At first, I couldn't understand what was happening, but when I finally accepted my fate, I had no mental or emotional capacity to move on. During the separation, my father asked me if I wanted to live with him, but I had no clue what to say.

When he finally left, I fell into depression. Not having him around all the time was devastating. I would miss his presence, scent, and voice always. I had no one to play hide-and-seek games with, nor could I ride someone's back. I lost all meaning to life. All those heartfelt conversations stopped as I couldn't express myself completely. I wanted my father back in my life. I wanted to see him more throughout the week; his visits were comforting, but they weren't enough to fill the growing emptiness I had inside me. As the clock ticked away, he started losing interest in us and I saw less of him. I didn't see him at all during my teen years. He grew distant and more temperamental over time.

Living with a single woman who raised two boys was tough. My mantra for calling my dad "Batman" changed to "Wonder Woman." This is the name I had given to my mom after I saw her working relentlessly to make ends meet. I saw her working through her pent-up emotions to provide us with a safe and healthy environment to grow up. Unfortunately, things weren't falling into place for me. I still missed having my dad around, but we were able to put the dark past behind us with time. He apologized for his behavior by telling me he couldn't move on from the trauma the separation caused him. I held his hand firm, hugged him tightly, and told him it was okay.

His eyes were teary and full of remorse, but I could sense something unreal flickering in his eyes. I wasn't sure if he meant what he said, I couldn't trust him anymore. As I hugged him, I couldn't sense anything mutual; he was cold like something was being forced on him. It was a façade; he didn't want me to stay in town and encouraged me to move from Miami. All my teen years, I was fighting for his acceptance, but at that moment, I realized that the only person I needed to accept was me, so I moved to Tampa, Florida, for a fresh start. My girlfriend then came with me, and I eventually made her my wife.

She was a part of our high school band; I saw her beautiful face when she played once and immediately thought she was the best-looking girl in the world. She belonged to an upper-middle-class family and lived in a posh locality. Her mom hosted parties for the entire neighborhood and shopped her heart out. They also used to travel a lot as a family. Not only did she have the latest cell phone in her class, but she also owned a car in the eleventh grade.

On the other hand, I was a shy guy back in high school. I didn't crave popularity or want a large group of friends. A few loyal friends would do for me, and I had the best three. They were the best trio. I noticed my ex-wife was not into me at all. She would move in large crowds and enjoy going to parties a lot. However, we started spending more time together when she moved to college. She told me her mother was giving her a hard time, and she soon started drifting away. I was familiar with this pain, so I could connect with her on a deeper level. That's what brought us together.

Maybe my strong urge to want to share her burden and free her from the pain encouraged me to propose to her, but, God, I wish I had waited and thought this over. The thought of supporting her through pain caused me to ignore all the red flags. I thought she was an intelligent, open-minded woman who started imposing rules on me. After work, I often played basketball outside with my friend, a lesbian. She was five foot five inches tall and had her hair styled with cornrows. She was easygoing and had been my friend before my marriage. I didn't want to lose her. My wife didn't want me to be friends with her. She used to say, "Married people need to hang out with married people."

I wouldn't say I liked her attitude because she wouldn't do the same. She was friends with the entire Tampa, Florida. I was cross with her; she had no right to persuade me to leave all my friends.

Soon, I heard the news of my father's murder, which crushed me. I was shattered to pieces, but I didn't express it in front of her as she was also dealing with the relationship with her parents' divorce. During that time, I can recall she also suffered a miscarriage, so I decided not to seek sympathy. I didn't wish to bother her.

I kept it all in me all these years. I put her comfort needs above mine, and in return, I got nothing. She didn't trust me being around my old friends. I started to budge here, I felt like she was controlling my entire life, and I wouldn't say I liked that. I couldn't have anyone telling me whom to keep around and whom not to, especially when she wasn't following this.

After suffering from this trauma, I became extremely unstable to the point where I failed miserably in my job. She expected me to follow by her rules but didn't follow her own rules. This is where our differences started to grow, and later, they resulted in conflicts. As time passed, we got tangled in our issues more to a point where everything seemed to spin out of control, and finally, the day came when we said goodbye to each other. I never imagined things would lead to this.

I got fired from my nine-year-old job over a stupid accident. While I was burning the midnight oil at a car wash to make ends meet, my wife was driving a brand-new vehicle. One night when I was finishing my rounds, I drove the truck through a one-way in and a one-way out of a narrow street with an unfinished road in south Georgia. My vehicle was overweight with liquor. As I made a right turn, my back tire hit the curb, causing the truck to get off the road and rollover. I lost my nine-year job just like that. Luckily, I had my second job, but I was still unable to pay for the mortgage, so I had to start all over again.

Back in Tampa, she had made friends with someone who would always look down on me and my achievements.

She was a negative person who ruined the peace of my home. She didn't want my wife to live with me because she was too caught up in her problems. She influenced my wife so negatively that she insisted on moving to Atlanta, Georgia.

Due to staying in her company for too long, my wife started insisting I move to Atlanta, Georgia. At first, I didn't want to, but eventually, I gave in to her whining. At this point in my life, I started thinking about children. I wanted to have a few, but my wife didn't. Whenever I would bring up the subject, she would change it or start doubting my intentions by asking questions like, "Are you sure? Why would I invite you to have them if I weren't ready? Do you think you are ready?"

I quit my previous job when we finally moved to Atlanta, Georgia. I was apprehensive about my new job as it didn't pay much, but I took it because I had no other option. I even bought a bigger house than we had in Tampa to give my wife the best life, but no matter what I did, it wasn't enough. When our fifth anniversary spruced up, she wanted a new wedding ring.

My father helped me pick the old one, so I was slightly upset. Why did she need a new one? Was the old one not good enough for her? Even though I was upset, I made the transaction and got her a new one. She didn't even have a stable job then, but I was with her through thick and thin. I helped her get around four different vehicles.

I did everything I could to give her a life filled with joy, comfort, and immense love, while she did the opposite. She ripped me of my peace, bruised my ego, and hurt my pride; I'll never forgive her. I could feel growing distance, not just from her but from myself. I could feel myself slipping from the cracks of her cold embrace. I lost my self-worth, couldn't recognize myself, and became unconscious over time; I had become rock solid like a hard block of ice lying aimlessly somewhere in its glory, not wanting to be cracked open. I missed my older self, but this is how you outgrow some parts of your life.

All I knew at this stage was that I had to move on, so I did. I went to live with a colleague who was caught up in his mess, away from my ex-wife. She brought me back to my high school self, the self-centered version of me that I had worked hard to get rid of. Looking back at it, I feel guilty, helpless, and traumatized. Finally, a part of me wants to apologize for leaving the way I did, but a part of me is satisfied because it was the right decision to make given that situation. I pray to God for peace, hope, and happiness.

CHAPTER 2

THE DIVORCE

"It is not a lack of love, but a lack of friendship that makes unhappy marriages."

—Friedrich Nietzsche

Generally, in deteriorating relationships, the responsibility for all emotional damage is put on the other person. One constantly gets blamed or overly criticized for their behavior when it should be distributed equally. Instead of playing the blame game on each other, it's better to opt for couples therapy and get your emotions sorted. When there is a lack of trust in marital life, self-doubt increases, making the relationship bitter.

Building a healthy bond with your spouse is evident, and trust is at its core. I feel the struggles I faced as a child; the trauma deeply rooted in me when I felt abandoned by my father negatively impacted my married life. My trust issues prevented me from making a genuine relationship with my spouse. For those planning to tie the knot shortly, my advice is to love and trust their spouse no matter what, and if you have unresolved trust issues, as I did, seek therapy to get yourself emotionally sorted before you marry someone.

Sometimes, people grow distant in marriage when they do things on their terms instead of listening to others.

Sometimes it can be the other way around, but that's where both partners need to understand the depth of the situation and try to get to the bottom. Even though I felt like we had a balance and many things in common, we stayed loveless for many years in our marriage.

Presenting yourself as highly intelligent or clever in front of your spouse is also considered toxic. When one of your spouses is dealing with vulnerability, and you aren't there emotionally for them, it increases anger toward each other, which later feeds off frustration, outbursts, and constant bickering.

These are the root causes of increased coercion, wrongful antics, misbehavior, and abuse. After this, the estrangement between the two families begins. When nobody takes control of their attitude, behavior, or aggression, the marriage starts to fall apart. It all starts with the little things. When you let go of the small things that bug you, a pile is created, which will eventually come crashing down someday. My purpose here is not to scare you off marriage but to educate you on addressing the little things that might cause significant trouble in the future.

For a successful marriage, it's evident that you self-reflect on your actions and behavior. When you are in touch with your thoughts, feelings, and emotions, you will be better at taking care of yourself and your better half. My marriage fell apart because my spouse would become overly critical of me. She would often pinpoint my actions as wrongful when she would be doing the same things. How was this fair on me? Who allowed her to bash, demean, and belittle me when she didn't apply her teachings to herself? To this day, I don't get why I was treated with so much disrespect. Why were my feelings not given importance when I kept hers as the foremost priority?

I clearly remember when I was struggling to cope with my father's murder, my wife had a miscarriage. I didn't want to inflict more pain on her by sharing my feelings. Instead, I suppressed my emotions and stayed quiet so as not to hurt her. This is what we call being considerate of your spouse's feelings. I knew if I had spilled my heart out, it would only make things worse for her, but when I expected her to do the same for me and show a little compassion, she did the complete opposite.

She doubted my intentions by accusing me of having an affair with my friend. I was forced to cut ties with my friend, who had been by my side during my tough times, only because my spouse didn't like her. She suggested I only talk to married people when she wouldn't do the same. Her continuous poking and opinionated behavior led to the decision to separate. I don't think she ever respected or accepted me for who I was. I was constantly compared to and looked down upon by her neighbor, whom she would invite for gossip sessions. I loathed her because she would belittle people who were college dropouts. I didn't like her energy in my house; my ex-wife knew. She would still do nothing.

If she had respected me, she would have stopped meeting her in the first place. She expected me to leave my friend when she wouldn't do the same for me. For me, this was quite hurtful. I couldn't handle this toxicity. I wanted to talk it out with her, but I knew deep down in my heart that she wouldn't listen. I don't think she honored me the way others would. I was a victim of inferiority in different ways. I was judged for my money, education, and family prestige.

Marriage partners tend to forget that the two are no longer separate; they are one now. Therefore, violating each other's dignity can be fatal for both. Mistakes are expected to happen in marital life; we are all human beings, but if they happen too often with no accountability, there could be more bumps and bruises. You must forgive the other person if your spouse has made a mistake. However, if you don't plan on doing that, give them space to rectify their behavior. You can always make them understand and help them meet you halfway, but that certainly takes up a lot of emotional and mental energy. However, couples should never delay the slightest confession to keep a marriage safe from falling apart. By establishing two channels of communication, they should always talk it out.

In my marriage, I felt a difference of opinion. I was being pushed to do something I didn't want to, such as moving to Atlanta. A partner should never force another partner toward something they don't desire. I would have appreciated it if she had discussed it before deciding. Her plan was not mine; I don't know why I was pushed into it. When faced with a difference in opinion, we may get defensive about our views and sometimes end up hurting the one in the process. This could be detrimental to any marital relationship, especially in the long run.

No conflicts can be resolved amicably with your spouse when you are at each other's neck fighting it out over a heated argument. Your mind becomes clouded by an overflow of thoughts, hindering your ability to think straight. Emotions run high and low during a disagreement. But instead of raising your voice or pointing fingers at each other, discussing feelings with your spouse is better.

Her tone would always tick me off. She would speak assertively, where you would feel the other person owns you. I found this highly disrespectful because I wouldn't do this to anyone. Even when people bring me down, I don't tend to lose respect for people who do me wrong. If their abominable behavior remained constant, I would distance myself from them first and then try to cut them off later. However, when your spouse makes your life miserable, how do you make it stop?

If she had taken things slowly by addressing her issues with me more maturely, I think it would have saved me from emotional damage. She could have gone about things the right way, but she didn't because she meant to hurt me on purpose. She planned on belittling me because it fed her ego. I wish I had known this narcissistic trait of hers before marrying her. My attempts to resolve the matter were always looked down upon. Sometimes, she would bring in past and unrelated events during an argument to cause more emotional turmoil.

Adopting a "give and take" approach should be a way of going about things, or an "agree to disagree" approach can help better sustain a relationship in the long run. We resolved the conflict well. I always tried to communicate my feelings so we wouldn't fight for a week. Whenever we crossed with each other for multiple days, that would take a toll on my mental health. I only enjoyed fighting with people for a short time. I always thought life to be a precious gift that was to be enjoyed. For me delving into negativity was not the way to pursue happiness and peace. I believed in the law of attraction very firmly.

Conjugating good thoughts and manifesting everything I

wanted from life was my ticket to success. Sure, there were hard times when I was expected to work long hours, but building a bankroll has always been one of my foremost priorities. I was a self-sufficient, hardworking fellow who tried to provide his spouse with an enriching life. However, unfortunately, my wife left no stone unturned in separating me from my finances. She didn't leave a single penny in my bank account.

One day, she got a new truck while I struggled to pay off the mortgage. She only cared about herself and her luxury. Not once did she ask me if it would be okay with me. How could she when I was barely making ends meet? Didn't she think about me once? How can someone be so insensitive? Right there, at that moment, I knew I needed a divorce from her. I couldn't provide her with the lifestyle she needed.

Your spouse is supposed to be your support system, someone who is emotionally available. Someone who puts your needs before themselves. I am willing to do that for my spouse, so why couldn't I get the same? Didn't I deserve happiness? Didn't I need a shoulder to cry on? A little sympathy? Where was my share of encouragement? I felt like I had always been alone while having my wife with me for years. When you reach that point in married life, you should opt for separation or split up.

We were recommended couples therapy, but that made things worse. My wife got an excuse to pour her heart out in front of a stranger and inform her how much she hated me. It broke me a lot more from the inside. Before going into couples therapy, I had decided to get divorced; nothing would help me change my mind. I am so glad I did. When I look back at my decision, I don't feel remorse. I don't have any regrets. God gave me the courage to step out of this toxic marriage; I am proud of myself for following my heart and grateful to God for helping me in every step.

CHAPTER 3

THE AFTERMATH OF DIVORCE

"Some things in my life are hard to reconcile, like divorce. Sometimes it is tough to understand how it could happen. Laying blame is so easy. I don't have time for hate or negativity in my life. There's no room for it."

—Reese Witherspoon

Losing your spouse to death is entirely different from losing them to divorce. When you lose your spouse over death, the expected emotional pain sucks your life out. There is a whole grieving process that is involved. It makes life confusing to both you and others. However, on the other hand, when people lose a spouse to divorce, many people find themselves on an ambiguous roadmap where they cannot process both the loss and their emotional turmoil. Some might find it hard to develop a new identity after separating from their spouses.

The relationship's disintegration and divorce can cause psychological distress that keeps you from moving forward. Some may feel regret, anxiety, resentment, confusion, fear, shame, and sadness during and after divorce. This could be heartbreaking and can cause significant damage to your emotional makeup, wreaking havoc on your mental and physical health. This can happen even if you were the one who decided to leave the marriage.

Deep emotional turmoil resulting from major life transitions is known as life-stage issues. Unlike spontaneous mental disorders, these psychological struggles are rooted in significant events that disrupt your ability to achieve emotional harmony and function healthily. Divorce is one of the most common stages of life's problems and is recognized by the Holmes and Rahe Stress Scale as the "second most stressful life event a person can experience after the death of a spouse." You may isolate yourself from family and friends, experience deep insecurities, act uncharacteristically destructive, have intrusive thoughts and overwhelming feelings of depression. Anxiety may arise preventing you from feeling joy or imagining a happy future.

As divorce becomes more common, the medical communities have recognized its devastating effects on physical and emotional well-being. Also, they have designed treatments specifically to help people struggling with divorce. These are some of the things I got to know after I filed for it. I suffered from depression in that marriage already, I figured maybe divorcing her would make things better, but it made it worse. I had no clue how tough it would be to process my emotions and live my life.

I filed for divorce when she bought a new truck for herself with our money. She knew I was struggling financially. That was the time I knew I had to leave. So, I talked to her, and we agreed on it. Initially, I was relieved but knew it would destroy me in a million pieces. Not letting these negative thoughts cloud my mind, I mustered up the courage to file for it no matter what. I figured out what would happen, but it wouldn't be as bad as I feel now. Maybe living alone would help me clear my mind and move past the years of trauma that I had received being with her. I am glad I didn't have any children with her. It's not that I didn't want a child; she was always against having children. You see, my needs and wants were never taken seriously. My feelings were dismissed whenever I tried to express them to my wife. She pretended to acknowledge them, but she was waiting for me to finish so she could carry on with her life. I was also not given the attention I needed and craved for some days. I mean, after all, we are all humans. We all need love, attention, comfort, and partner support. Isn't this what companionship is all about?

Whatever decision you make during difficult times, please give them a long thought before you implement them, and once you have taken them, there is no going back. Be ready to go through some extremely traumatic events after you separate from your spouse. Trauma changes the chemistry in your body. Your body is flooded with adrenaline and cortisol, the stress hormones. You will feel your heart rate and blood pressure go up. This never helps you develop emotionally. You get ready to run away from your responsibilities and fight only for survival. Get away from this flight-fight-freeze response to every given threat and situation.

Do we get married to live a hyper-independent life where we must care for ourselves alone, or do we get married to someone who is supposed to look out for us? Companionship fills the void of loneliness that we all tend to develop over the years. But what is its use if you feel the same way in a marriage? Aren't you two better off alone?

One of the cruelest aspects of mental illness is that it robs us of any ability to believe that other people could suffer as we do. We are not intentionally self-centered or arrogant; our diseases make us feel extraordinarily pathetic, unacceptable, and awful. Our psychological problems clothe us in terrifying degrees of shame. Sick, we start running away from others.

Gatherings become impossible because we preemptively become frightened by our perceived vulnerability and judgment of those we might encounter. There is no way we can make small talk or focus on what someone else is saying when our heads are full of disaster scenarios and an intrusive voice tells us we will die. There doesn't seem to be any compact or acceptable way to share what we've been through with old friends: they knew us to be talkative and upbeat. What would they do with the tortured characters we've become? We began to assume that no one on earth could ever know, let alone accept, what it was like to be us.

The reason why someone feels isolated or lonely can vary depending on their circumstance and environment. Companionship is a basic human need and creates a sense of belonging. A life partner, whether a family member, friend, or caregiver, helps keep you mentally active and prevents social isolation. Someone to start a conversation with, even for a few moments, promotes mental stimulation, positive thinking, and memory retrieval. If you have someone you trust, you can also have honest conversations about how you feel. Whether it's about emotions, mental health, or illness, having someone to talk to can keep people from feeling alone.

Of course, when you are very young, your most important social relationship is with your parents or caregivers. But as children go to school, they begin to form deeper friendships that involve doing things together and a more profound shared emotional element. It then becomes even more abstract and relational during adolescence.

As a teenager, your brain is tuned to social cues and connections like never before. During high school and college, friendships can seem easy because they put you in an environment where you are many of your age and are a circle of potential friends. They are very interested in social activities.

Later, in adulthood, spending time with friends can be more difficult when people start working and getting married or starting a family. Toward the end of life, we tend to have a little more time again when the children are older, and our career or job is less demanding.

There are those transitional points in life where it's easier or more challenging to spend time with friends, but people need to know that friendship is a lifelong endeavor and that it's something people should be mindful of in all aspects of life. People sometimes (especially in their 30s and 40s) think, "I don't have time for friends right now," and that's a mistake.

When you turn sixty-five and are ready to pay attention to your friends, that's like retiring at sixty-five. If you go from fifteen to sixty-five and always smoke, quitting is still better, but some damage will be done. And if you're not paying attention to friends all the time, the same applies.

Friendship is one of the hallmarks of a happy and lasting marriage and the foundation of a healthy marriage. Research has shown that couples who are close friends have higher overall marital satisfaction rates. The emotional connection between married couples is said to be five times more important than their physical intimacy. Friend couples look forward to spending time together and liking each other. Their activities and interests improve because they have their favorite person to share their life experiences with.

Establishing and maintaining marital friendship can strengthen a marriage since company in marriage is known to build emotional and physical intimacy. Therapy helps married couples feel safe enough to be more open with each other without worrying about being judged or feeling insecure. Nurturing and building that friendship in a marriage takes practice and time and effort. Unfortunately, in my marriage, it was always one-sided. No matter how I tried to save us from divorce, it couldn't work. One person cannot save the marriage. This may be harsh, but it is true.

I have news for those who believe they alone can save their entire marriage: "It's not going to work out." Stop being a punching bag and start setting some boundaries for yourself. You cannot help someone who doesn't want to help themselves. Start taking control of your life to win in every situation. What's done is done; there is no point in waiting for something special to happen. Collect all the pieces there are left of you and move out. This is the best thing you can do for yourself. You are not a doormat.

CHAPTER 4
THE THERAPIST

In my case, getting into a relationship with my therapist was the biggest mistake I had ever made in my entire life. It was the time when I had moved out of my home and lived with my coworker. While my wife used to drive me to these sessions in her new truck, I was going to them for the sake of it. I knew these sessions could not do anything good for me. The damage had already been done. I remember I would work out a lot as it kept my mind off my ex-wife. I figured being physically fit would help me grasp some control over my emotions. I must be out of my mind.

My therapist and I would talk about a lot of personal issues. I felt comfortable opening up to her as she was my therapist. I thought to myself, "What harm could it cause?" Little did I know, I was dragging myself to doom. Her presence made me feel safe, but it was not enough to move in with someone. She would often bring her six-year-old son to these sessions. Since I have always longed for a family, I became close to them. After spending time together, we reached a point where she asked me to move in with her and her children. Sure, we could make unforgettable memories together, but those were short-lived.

Right after moving in, I didn't want to put a label on our relationship, but she stated it to be a committed relationship. I didn't know her well enough; we were simply friends then. This was the time I started to see red flags. Not only was she six years older than me, but her habit of making decisions for us baffled me beyond my imagination. She already knew about my upbringing and past life, but I had no intention of tying the knot with this woman, especially when I was still not over my ex-wife. A few months after moving in with her, I discovered she was still married to her husband. She told me she would get divorced but never filed for one while we were still together. This unfortunate series of events shattered me into a million pieces.

Her family would always take her side even when she was wrong. After being submerged in this pool of trauma, I gradually realized. I concluded that stability didn't matter to anyone. She didn't care with whom she lived or about giving her children a peaceful life. She had not developed a meaningful relationship with any man in her life. I pity myself for even thinking I could become integrated into her life. People who aren't sincere with their loved ones don't deserve peace and happiness.

My mother fought hard for her children even when her marriage went down. She had refused to give up.

Building and living in a stable environment matters where a person's emotional well-being is cared for. It isn't enjoyable to think that, for some people, a person's emotional development doesn't matter. Well, I could not have it anymore. I had to end this because it was driving me insane. When I got divorced, I gave everything to my ex-wife, so I had nothing to offer her, but I knew I had determination, drive, structure, and self-respect in who I was as a man. I was starting from scratch when we met. I was at ground zero! And that was why I initially did not want to move in with her. I overheard a conversation she was having with one of her friends on the phone. She stated that she was doing everything around the house to keep it together, including paying all the bills, and that she was broke. I realized then why her friends would always look at me in disgust as if I wasn't doing my part as a man.

We started dating in 2018; however, I didn't have a job, and she knew that when she asked me to move in. I was searching for a job everywhere! I had submitted applications to all the job sites and even walked around to stores handing out my application, and I was waiting for someone to hire. I would go home daily with shattered self-esteem and pretend nothing had happened. I tried to foster a positive environment for the children, including her.

We also had severe financial issues, as I was unemployed then.

She always convinced me to use her EBT card, but I was against this idea. I knew I had to find a job and become financially independent. Eventually, I did, and it was terrific. It was at a detention center where I cared for mentally ill kids I taught and spent much time with. I often argued with my therapist's girlfriend as my new job was demanding. However, I enjoyed being away from home. Did I mention she accused me of cheating most of the time? Whenever my study buddy would call, she would think we were having an affair. I was stressed out so much that I failed my class and had to start over again.

Sometimes, we would argue over something as stupid as not being too grateful. I left when she finally pushed me to the limit where I couldn't take it. That night I drove to my cousin's house for two days. I then received a phone call claiming she was pregnant with my child. Although I should have been unhappy, tears started rolling down my eyes. I couldn't wait for the newborn to arrive. I had finally gotten my wish of having a baby.

On April 20, 2020, she began to have labor pain. Even though we weren't together, I promised her that I would be there no matter what; I didn't want to miss the birth of my child. I knew deep down inside my relationship wouldn't last, but I had to be there for my newborn. I didn't want her to come into this world without me being on her side. There were numerous occasions when I was not heard or spoken to. Conversations were left unsaid, meetings were left unattended, and our relationship was left mangled. There were no efforts from the other side for any amendments. I was left in a dark place with no trust in myself.

If I hadn't left, I wouldn't have been able to write this book. I would have lost my complete self. I am grateful to God that I did not reach a point where I couldn't recognize myself. This is the exact message, my story, that I want to convey to my readers. I want them to stay clear of such toxicity in their life. It's good to keep yourself a priority, focus on your mental health, and free yourself from the façade. It is liberating! So, whenever you feel tormented by a bond you thought was out of this world, think again.

CHAPTER 5
CO-PARENTING WITH A NARCISSIST

Having a child is one of God's greatest blessings. I can never say that I am ungrateful for my daughter. She is the best thing that has ever happened to me. Even though she was born in times quite dark for me, there is nothing I would not do for her in this world. She was everything perfect you can imagine.

There were many tantrums and feuds that I had to deal with right after my daughter came into this world from the therapist. You see, when there is someone as toxic as the therapist in your life, it gets tricky for anyone to enjoy the special moments. When I look back and think of the day my daughter was born, I can't recall experiencing tranquility. Instantly, somebody snatched the little amount of joy I participated in. Her mother showed me an attitude, not wanting me to come near my daughter or her ex-husband.

Those were tough times; sometimes, I would stare into the abyss, thinking of what I did to deserve so much torment. Where did I go wrong in treating people? Why am I not receiving the same love from them? Am I a pushover? A cauldron of such thoughts would simmer in my mind all day long. I would become emotionally exhausted and mentally drained. My work life and personal life were both getting affected by this. There was something that needed to be done.

People tend to see themselves as victims in every situation. If they mess up, they might shift the blame to someone else or tell a story that paints them more positively. Sometimes, when I would call my therapist out on her behavior, she would pull out old screenshots indicating when I had been rude to her. If you study psychology in detail, you will know that only that person with narcissistic traits does this. They would use the deflecting method by bringing up old things from the past instead of discussing issues at hand.

During an argument, they would either try to divert from the subject or have an angry outburst. I suggest ending the conversation at once. This is the safest option because the conversation needs to be led somewhere.

Dealing with someone's toxic behavior can be exhausting. The person might become overly critical of your behavior, coming up with a new story about unfair treatment or even accusing you of doing them wrong. They will turn your words on you. During these times, you can always respond with a simple, "I am sorry you feel that way," and leave it at that. Don't even apologize; say you are not up for this conversation.

If you aren't aware of how the other person is treating you, become more aware of how they are making you feel. That can help you better navigate interactions with them. Please pay attention to how their tone gets when they become offensive. Take notes and start taking action.

It would be best to get serious when the other person puts you down, lies, or uses different kinds of emotional and verbal abuse. Do they apologize or seem to notice how what they say or do affects you? So, why should you care? Do everything in your power to protect your mental health. If you won't take a stand for yourself, then who would?

People who are narcissists will throw love bombs at you first and then stop suddenly, making you crave that attention. The continuous patterns of affection and detachment will make you addicted to them. This will happen so fast that you won't even realize what they are doing to you. Sooner and later, you will find yourself roaming around them, trying to seek validation.

Sometimes toxic people will trap you like you are prey to them. You know you don't have to give in to them, but you also know there will be consequences if you don't—the secret to deciding from a position of power rather than feeling controlled.

Just as they want something from you, there will always be something you want from them (even if it's to avoid further toxicity).

Decide that you are doing what you do to control them and their behavior, not because you are a victim of their manipulation. Personal power has everything to do with what you believe and nothing with what you think.

Toxic people will always see in others what they don't want to acknowledge about themselves. It is called projection. You could be the kindest, most generous, and most hardworking person on the planet, and toxic people will turn against you, trying to convince you that you are a liar. You are unfair, evil, or lazy. See it for what it is. You know the truth, even if they will never know.

Think about it like this: imagine a child throwing a tantrum. If you persevere and refuse to give up, he will try harder for a while. We all tend to do that when something we're doing stops working. Toxic people are no different. Once they have found a way to control and manipulate you and it no longer works, they will do more than they used to before retreating and finding another target. Please do not take his escalation as a stop sign. Please take this as a sign that you are teaching them their old behavior will no longer work. Give them time to convince themselves you are not hanging around on your decision to turn them off.

It would help if you also were clear about boundaries. You can't please everyone, but toxic people make you think you can. They will somehow make you believe this.

It is exhausting when you are around them.

You don't realize you had one.

Knowing what you do and don't tolerate, you can decide how far you're willing to let someone push your boundaries before it's no longer worth it. Get ready to listen to that inner voice telling you something is wrong.

Refrain from falling under the deception of thinking whether the actions of others are right or wrong. Remember, whether you believe it's right or wrong is the only thing that matters. You need to deal with the situation by keeping your perspective in place. I would have lost my daughter instantly if I hadn't done that.

The therapist's ex-husband came back into the picture shortly after the birth of my daughter. Before this, he was nowhere to be seen. Isn't it ironic that people suddenly show up from nowhere, only to intrude in your life and make it more miserable? Wasn't the therapist enough to make my life a living hell already?

He would often interfere in my dealings regarding my daughter. Did he not know she was my daughter and not his? Did I need to remind him again? I mean, what an idiot!

I tried to find joy by being with my daughter, but that was not enough to fill the void inside my heart. I was going to need more time to complete myself.

My financial issues were piling up, on the other hand. After I served her the second time, she made a schedule containing time slots to meet my daughter. But guess what? They all matched her plan, not mine. Deep down inside, I could see this coming. She refused to go along with the e-schedule she made. The day I was supposed to spend time with my daughter, she would come up with excuses, so I could not meet her.

Christmas had just passed, and driving an hour to her house was draining me. So, I decided to accept her decision and wait patiently for court. However, fortunately, God made way for me to see my child for a second on the day she refused to let me see her child.

It happened when I took an Uber around four in the morning. I would pick up a young guy who took forever to leave the house. I waited patiently and saw that I had to drop him off at a church. I noticed he had brought a piano when he got into the car. He was very upbeat. When we got to the church, I waited for the next ride. Then in the spur of the moment, someone came to the window and said, "I knew this was your car."

She was an active member of the church. I tried not to create a scene. I looked and drove off, but I thought about my little girl. So, I stopped and saw her husband get her out of the car seat. Nevertheless, I spoke, and he thought I was picking her up, but it was a coincidence that I was at the right place and time.

I wanted to hold my daughter for a moment before she went inside the church. It was not a big thing I was asking for. As soon as I reached my daughter to hold her in my arms, the therapist came closer, wanting to snatch her away, but I stood my ground this time. I knew exactly what I wanted and was not going to back down. Her husband then backed up, put his earphones on, and ignored the situation his wife was creating. Honestly, I have no respect for this man.

When I discussed this with a friend, she told me you couldn't expect people to have a good understanding of who you are when they refused to see the best in you. Getting a grip on my anger, I kissed my baby girl goodbye, and she started crying for me, which hurt me the most. I then gave her to her mother. At this point, I wasn't even mad at her for being the narcissist she was. I was numb to her evil ways already. It didn't affect me how it used to affect me.

Narcissistic people think the entire world revolves around them, but there is a limit to everything. She wanted me to feel bad, cry, beg, and plead for my baby girl, but I wasn't going to throw in the towel right now. I was going to fight until the last breath. She wasn't going to win this time; I wasn't going to let her.

She wanted to dominate me, but this time I was coming out stronger. I understand she was raised differently and wasn't happy in her marriage, but that gave her no right to throw me under the bus completely. I believe karma hits everyone in the face. If you do wrong to others, you will get smashed in the face sooner or later. Things might not work out for you. You will be in shallow waters.

When you see dishonest and cruel people in positions of power advancing in life or kind people in need dying young, you may find it difficult to believe in karma. Many people only invest in karma in times of need or when uncontrollable situations arise, such as deteriorating health.

Someone who gossips, manipulates others, or creates dramatic situations might not realize how their behavior affects you or anyone else. An open conversation may help them recognize that this behavior is unacceptable. You need to be careful with your energy in this world, or someone will come along and snatch everything away from you.

If you have a dream, you need to protect it. It would help if you were mindful of the people you allow in your life, or else this cruel world will take everything from you, and trust me, you will be left with nothing. So, stop wasting your energy on what doesn't matter and start spending it on things that add value to your life.

CHAPTER 6
MY DAUGHTER, MY HEARTBEAT

Even though I wasn't around her much, my daughter filled my life with beauty and joy. The best part was that I knew this was going to happen. My heart could feel the gift of life I was about to get blessed with, and when she was finally here, I could feel serendipity in every bone of my body.

After all the hardships, God showed me hope through her. God was watching over me, as he had always been on my side. I felt rejuvenated like something was igniting my bones, showing me the silver lining behind the dark clouds that I had been surrounded with all these years, like someone held my hand tightly, with no intention of letting it go.

The benevolence you feel when your newborn comes into your hands stays with you forever, changing you forever. My daughter is fantastic, and she is everything a father could ask for. She is my heart, my soul, and everything in between. My days are incomplete without her. She makes me believe in myself. She is the source of my laughs; my little moments of life are filled with happiness whenever I am with her. She has the personality of a feisty three-year-old who knows precisely what she wants.

I have observed people often thinking of their daughters as burdens. How can such beautiful creatures cause trouble to anyone? I don't understand. If you have ever been blessed with a daughter, I suggest you hold onto this blessing tightly. Having a baby is the utmost blessing for those who believe in God. It should never be taken for granted.

God gives a child to a family when he wants to take things further. He places responsibility on them by ensuring the parents provide for their children. I don't get people who consider their children a stream of extra expenses or a burden on the family. They would have to work tirelessly, challenging in the modern age, to ensure they have a roof over their head, food in their stomach, and access to quality education.

Now that we are progressing into a new world, daughters are equal to their sons. They can achieve everything a man can if we give them the proper education, encouragement, and support.

We should see babies as a blessing and look forward to enjoying the experience. Not just having a baby but having a family is a benediction. Both are interrelated with each other. Bringing up a child is considered tough and challenging in the modern age, but is it? I want you all to stop thinking about this for a moment.

I believe it's becoming essential to change our society and their mentality of not investing enough time in their children. We must evolve our perspectives on parenting, ensuring both parents take a leading role in their child's development. Kids are deemed a financial burden by their parents instead of becoming economic support. This appears to be an antecedent mindset that children are troublesome, inconvenient, violent, or extravagant.

People don't understand that giving birth to a child is unrivaled. Even though my daughter was not brought into this world in the best circumstances, I tried my best to be with her. I wanted her to have a fulfilling life. Knowing the therapist's husband came into the picture, I strived to fight for my daughter's future. I didn't want her to be thrown back and forth between two houses like a paper bag. What kind of impact could this have on her young mind? She would be heartbroken. A safe home environment is crucial for a child's stable upbringing. Their primary caregivers are the only ones who can provide that. I know her primary caregivers were together, but that didn't mean we had vague intentions regarding raising her.

I was ready to fight for my daughter's rights. She wasn't going to grow up without her biological father. The father who created her. I know my daughter's mother had a lot against me. Praying every night, wishing for this nightmare to end, the therapist and her husband inflicted so much pain that I would never respect them.

Fighting my inner rage that had been building up and preparing a case for my daughter to win custody was a tormenting job. Not only was it mentally exhausting, but it was also emotionally draining. Whenever I thought about giving up, I would picture my daughter's beaming face. It would soothe my heart, making my worries melt away. After thinking of her for a while, I would muster up the courage to get back on track and make an impeccable defense.

The first time I served her, she convinced me we could do it without the courts. She told me how important it is to act like an adult and not publicize private affairs. I was gullible, so I moved ahead with it. She gaslighted me through her evil, manipulative ways. She was a therapist, so she knew her way around other people's psychology. She understood the techniques she could use to twist my mind in a way that offered convenience to her. I regretted doing it because I should have known better. However, it opened my eyes more because I knew she could not be trusted now.

So, you can say it was a blessing in disguise. From my point of view, I became more aware of the tricks to watch out for in the future. I was coming out to be stronger and more cunning. Feeling more powerful than ever before, I started recognizing courage in me that I didn't know was their back. Maybe it was God who had given me this faith or the harsh life lessons I had faced my entire life. Whatever it was, I felt as if I had been reborn. I was a whole new person.

This new person didn't know failure; he didn't know how to back down. I was unstoppable now. I was going to fight for my daughter through thick or thin now. It was that therapist against me. She wasn't going to win this time.

CHAPTER 7
PROTECTING YOUR CHILDREN'S MENTAL HEALTH

There was one thing I realized while fighting for my child's custody that your children's mental health should be kept as the utmost priority. I believe every child to be precious; they are impressionable and fragile. You would be best if you did everything possible; they can protect them, especially when fighting over their custody. Putting them in the middle of the feud will only wreck their mental peace. It should be kept private as much as possible, so they are not emotionally affected.

Any child can become withdrawn during a child custody battle in no time. It can impact their academics in staggering ways. If they're children, you might notice they might stop talking to their parents. They might become isolated and more inclined toward spending time alone. Worst-case scenario, they might develop clinical depression over time.

Their tendency not to be able to maintain mental peace might hurt their physical health. They might go a day without eating or drinking. Their entire body nourishment might suffer. Some might even start developing suicidal thoughts. We as parents need to end this suffering, but I know it's not as easy as it seems.

Children develop signs of aggressive behavior when their emotional needs are not met. They might completely shut their complete self or start acting out in school. Their grades might also suffer. Some might even become violent. We don't know how their peers might react to their parents' divorce, so these matters should be kept private.

Going through such an emotional issue early in life can wind up scaring them for a long time. Some parents might think their toddlers or infants may not suffer from trauma as they cannot understand the situation, but unfortunately, that's not the case.

Young children may also experience traumatic stress in response to painful medical procedures or the sudden loss of a parent/caregiver.

A growing body of research has established that young children may be affected by events that threaten their safety or the safety of their parents/caregivers, and their symptoms have been well documented. These traumas can result from intentional violence, such as physical or sexual abuse or domestic violence or natural disasters, accidents, or war. Young children also may experience traumatic stress in response to painful medical procedures or the sudden loss of a parent/caregiver.

Going through such emotional turmoil can give them a negative view of life. A two-year-old witnessing a traumatic event when his mother is being battered may interpret it differently than a five-year-old or an eleven-year-old. Children may blame themselves or their parents for failing to prevent or change the outcome of a frightening event. These misconceptions about reality amplify the adverse effects of trauma on children's development.

Young children who experience trauma are at a greater risk because their rapidly developing brains are vulnerable. Early childhood trauma has been associated with reduced cerebral cortex size.

This area is primarily responsible for many complex functions, including memory, attention, perceptual awareness, thinking language, and consciousness. These significantly affect IQ and the ability to regulate emotions. The child may become more anxious and less safe or secure.

Young children depend solely on parents/carers for their survival and protection, both physically and emotionally. If the trauma also affects the parent/carer, the relationship between that person and the child can be severely affected.

Without the support of a trusted parent/caregiver to help them regulate their powerful emotions, children can experience over-whelming stress with little ability to communicate what they are feeling or need effectively. They often develop symptoms that parents/carers do not understand and may exhibit unusual behaviors that adults cannot understand and know how to respond to appropriately.

CHAPTER 8

PROTECTING YOUR MENTAL HEALTH

A custody case is an ordeal that should not be faced alone. The emotional toll can be overwhelming, so finding someone who has been through it to help you express your feelings should be a priority. The support of friends and family can bring clarity during difficult times and means you will be better prepared to raise your children from an emotionally aware perspective.

You can rely on various support networks if you don't have friends or family to help you with your stress. For example, support groups provide a safe space to share your experiences with people who understand what you are going through and can provide invaluable information.

If sharing with a group isn't for you and you prefer a one-on-one environment, a qualified therapist can help you process any feelings accompanying a custody battle.

HAVE A PLAN

It's easy to get caught up in the emotions of a custody trial, but it's in your children's best interests to stay in control. While this is easier said than done, experts say that paying attention to you and your co-parent's actions can ease the emotional aspect.

Instead of letting feelings dominate, record interactions and behaviors so you can jot them down and then focus on what matters most.

Just being angry or reactive causes nothing but extra stress. You break this habit by nipping anger in the bud by tracking behaviors and events. Not only will this help you, but an organized record of important details will show any court that you are competent and conscientious and will give you an advantage during a court proceeding.

TAKE CARE OF YOURSELF

A custody case is both physically and mentally demanding. You want to win if self-care isn't a priority, but it will be an empty tank. How can you expect to fight for your child when struggling with it? If you spend the energy you have left on the wrong things, for instance, overthinking or focusing on the past will fuel the flames of your fear.

Refocus that energy instead. The energy within yourself to become the best parent who can eat well, be physically active, and sleep well. Whether you physically use this energy (e.g., boxing to release pent-up frustrations or meditating in a quiet environment to clear your mind), you address the effects of this combat charge and ensure the process is so much easier to deal with.

COMMUNICATION IS KEY

Except in extreme cases where parents must lose touch, ceasing communication with your spouse essentially means ending the possibility of co-parenting, something your children need during this confusing time. This cannot be easy and often depends on your spouse's will. Still, open communication and mutual respect are critical to maintaining a safe and nurturing environment for your children.

PUT YOUR CHILDREN'S NEEDS FIRST

The process of a custody case is so overwhelming for children that both parents must be available to provide the care they need at that time. Focusing on the case might seem like the best option for your future, but it may mean you lose sight of what's important now.

To stay connected and present with your children, try to stay in touch with them, their lives, and their daily routines. You may not always feel like it, but you control the situation and your actions. Use every opportunity to facilitate the process for your children while maintaining boundaries and structure. If possible, have a plan with your co-parent for this.

Create a safe space for your child to feel how they need to and give them the freedom to ask questions about the situation.

FIND YOURSELF A GOOD LAWYER

Giving up control is never easy, especially when your children's well-being is at stake, but it's best to have someone with much experience on your side in these cases. No two cases are alike, so hiring an attorney who understands your needs and challenges and can negotiate to relieve tension between you and your spouse is essential.

The amount of paperwork and a long list of court dates can seem overwhelming while working to maintain structure and stability in your children's lives. You cannot be expected to attend to the business side of their case. Being a good father just isn't enough in court. You need someone with extensive experience to tell a judge that you are the fittest parent to provide your children with the best possible home.

Taking on this burden will inevitably lead to increased stress and anxiety, which will put you at a disadvantage in your efforts to raise your children and win your case. No one should go through this alone. Maintaining the right mindset goes hand in hand with always hiring the right representative to be by your side.

AVOID SOCIAL MEDIA

Nothing is private online. A profile set to private may feel safe, but screenshots can be taken by other parties without your knowledge and used in court. The post you shared that seems innocent may tell a different story.

For example, your spouse may use a selection of photographs of you having a soft drink or two to demonstrate to a judge that you are an inappropriate parent with a drinking problem.

It can also be tempting to tell friends and supporters of your situation, but that can quickly backfire. If you are unsure about posting, consider a general guide beforehand. Think about what you want to share; if you don't want it to become public in court, it's best not to post.

I always kept my affairs personal; there was no point in sharing them online or making a fuss about them in my family. I did it to protect my daughter's privacy. There was no way I was going to let them ruin that. While fighting for her custody, there was a new thing I learned every day.

Some days I found myself confident, driven, and focused on my goal. At the same time, some mornings, I would feel emotionally drained, like a bucket load of anxiety, depression, and disappointment had been unleashed on me. Some nights I would toss and turn in bed, unable to fall asleep. Whenever I fell asleep, I would wake up in the middle of the night gasping for breath, looking for hope. I wanted these dark clouds that were descended upon me to be gone. I could not take it anymore, but there was one thing I was sure of; God was watching me and my little angel.

He wanted to reunite us; there was no other way about it. God was not going to abandon me. He would get me out of this bottomless dark pit of wallowing and self-pity. He was going to rescue me. I had to rely on him because he was my only savior. I had to hold on to my faith a bit longer. God has gotten me this far; I would not back down now.

You might feel pity for me after reading my story and knowing me on a deeper level, but I don't want that to happen. The only reason behind jotting down my entire life story is that

I want you to learn real-life lessons from it. I wish to become an inspiration for all single fathers, mothers, or people in general who are fighting for their child's custody.

This battle can be long and hard, knocking you to the ground, but the journey will be worth every effort and tear. So, don't give up! You are closer to your destination than you think. Thoughts of throwing in the towel might interfere with your productivity but don't ever listen to that voice.

Leap of solid belief in yourself, keep your head strong, and fight.

CHAPTER 9
THE BATTLE FOR YOUR CHILD

Child custody battles can be traumatizing for children. They trigger all kinds of emotional pain along with a mountain of unsettling feelings. It disrupts the life you know and launches you into uncharted territory.

Everything around you tend to change; your routine, regime, ability to trust someone, and the loss of your self-esteem are significant. It would be best if you also were more particular about the future. You start to lose faith in the Almighty, and your courage is damaged. You feel trapped in time, wanting to escape from the situation to a place with hope, prosperity, and tranquility. However, the harsh reality keeps hitting you like a bus crushing you under its tires. No matter how hard you try to escape these circumstances, it's soul-crushing.

The emotional rollercoaster one goes through during these challenging times is unforgettable. They can wreck years of built self-esteem, attitude, and confidence. Along these lines, you may be blown away by how devastated you always feel. Allowing yourself to feel your emotions and move through the pain of your losses is what can help you let go of your worries. It would be best if you processed your emotions. That is the only way to experience life and move on.

There are many of you out there who would suppress your feelings or run away from feeling them. This is the worst thing you can do to yourself. You must take the time out and let your emotions run through your system. Also, engaging in healthy activities like working out might relieve all the emotional frustration. You need to be patient and work your way through life. There is no need to act strong consistently; feeling lost, broken, or shattered from the inside is okay. That makes us human. You are not in competition with someone, this is your life, and you need to take full responsibility for it. You can start by taking small steps toward healthy habits. For instance, adopting techniques and habits that allow you to become mentally stable or taking a day off from work can do wonders.

Here are a few ways you can stay strong in a challenging situation.

ACCEPT THAT SOME SITUATIONS ARE BEYOND YOUR CONTROL

If you type in "how to stay strong in tough times" an internet search bar, you will see the phrase "Accept the reality" pop up just about everywhere. Whether it's the advice of a psychologist or someone sharing their harrowing experience, it's the first thing we should do to gather our inner strength.

Easier said than done, of course. There's a reason acceptance is the final stage of grief. We must go through our other emotions before we get to this point. Denial, anger, frustration, and disappointment all play a role in finding acceptance. Therefore, identify the problem and try to understand its root cause. After you have ultimately decided to accept it, move ahead.

ALLOW YOURSELF TO FEEL

Death has no exclusive right to mourning. In other words, one does not have to experience death to validate their right to mourn. Any loss, be it a human being, a beloved pet, or even your life savings, can cause grief. So, get angry whenever you feel like it. Call upon the universe or those in power that you will do whatever it takes to reverse this tragedy. Once you've gone through your feelings (possibly multiple times), you are willing to accept that there are things you can't control in this world and find the strength to deal with them.

There's a scene in an episode of Mr. Rogers where he's trying to set up a tent. He wrestles with it for about a minute, then says, "I guess it takes two adults to hold on." In the Tom Hanks film, the producer tells Mr. Rogers they can cut or install it beforehand.

Even adults sometimes need to hear this message. Being strong doesn't mean you never need help. But on the contrary, it is understandable that sometimes we cannot do everything independently. Realizing that some problems are too big for a single person is one of the best ways to stay strong in difficult times.

WHENEVER POSSIBLE, OFFER HELP TO THOSE IN NEED

Helping others overcome tough times isn't just good for the soul; it's a brilliant way to help yourself stay strong. A 2015 Association for Psychological Science study found that helping friends, family, or strangers can "mitigate the impact of daily stressors on our emotions and mental health." It's hard to find the strength to help others when you feel like you can't help yourself.

Here, you don't have to make big gestures to make sense. Minor acts of kindness can go a long way in creating a better world and a strong person. Even sending a heartfelt email to a lonely friend can help lift your spirits and make you feel stronger. When you realize you have a plan, you also find the power to help yourself.

TAKE JOY WHERE LIFE OFFERS IT

We've talked about this a lot lately, but it needs to be repeated. It would be best to take advantage of life's joy to stay strong in difficult times. A starry night, a bright flower, a bird singing outside your window, a baby's hysterical laughter—if you look, you'll find joy everywhere.

You can clear your mind fully by avoiding these small pleasures and concentrating solely on what is wrong. When anything goes wrong, we frequently believe that grinning would be rude, and we shouldn't do it. When people are dying, how can we laugh at a humorous show? Nevertheless, spending some time for yourself doesn't imply ignoring or turning a blind eye to the issue. Trust me, it doesn't.

I want all parents fighting for their children's custody to stay vigilant of the challenges this battle will bring. Not only their mental health is at risk, but their children might suffer from it immensely.

According to a study by the California Cognitive Behavior Institute, children are affected in various ways and often go through stages like grieving the loss of a loved one. The parent's relationship, how much conflict they have, or how well they have communicated directly affects a child's psychological response.

> **Denial:** Young children are particularly prone to make-up fantasies.
>
> **Abandonment:** Children fear abandonment just as quickly as their parents fear it. This can be especially damaging if the children are not given "permission" to have a relationship with the other parent.
>
> **Preoccupation with Information:** Children want to know details. Removing children from circumstances might seem like a way to protect them, but studies have shown that children are more likely to get answers from their parents than when parents keep the line of communication open.
>
> **Hostility and Anger:** Children who don't know how to deal with anger may take it out on friends, family, or school. This inner anger is often depression.
>
> **Depression:** Some children become disengaged from activities they once enjoyed, become socially withdrawn, and in extreme cases, may physically harm themselves.
>
> **Immaturity of Over-maturity:** Some children might wet the bed or talk like babies, while others seem to fit into a more adult role, focusing on the emotional needs of the parents rather than themselves.
>
> **Concern:** Sometimes, when there is a conflict between parents, the children tend to cling to reconciliation and do not accept separation.

Acting Out: Children can absorb their parent's anger and will vent it in a refusal to speak to the "blame" parents or in parent-like behavior. If a parent is irate, their child will imitate.

Try putting the needs of children first. Try thoroughly assessing their moods and emotions and giving them the necessary space.

Unfortunately, child custody is the area of divorce practice that tends to cause the most heated controversy.

CONTACT A CHILD ATTORNEY

When it comes to custody disputes, it is often against the parents. Numerous gender stereotypes work against fathers in all family law matters but seem particularly pronounced in custody matters.

Unfortunately, child custody is the area of divorce practice that tends to cause the most heated controversy. Divorce can affect almost every aspect of your life, but issues like the division of assets and spousal support pale compared to your relationship with your children. Too often, fathers are relegated to a secondary parenting role when custody is decided.

If you're a parent facing a divorce and custody battle, it's best to be prepared for what lies ahead.

PAY ATTENTION TO THE DETAILS

Whether you seek sole or joint custody, showing that you are involved and committed to your child's life is essential. That means knowing everything from your child's class schedule to the names of their best friends.

As her father, you probably already know this information but don't leave it to chance. A judge can tell the difference between a father who is intimately involved in his child's life and a father who is a passive participant in it.

DON'T CONFIDE IN YOUR CHILD

Divorce is so emotionally challenging that many parents are

desperate for a listening ear to vent their frustrations. But no matter how stressful your divorce is or how frustrated you are with your ex, don't bitch or rave about your child.

Throwing your ex out in the trash in front of your child can potentially lead to parental alienation, which is incredibly damaging.

It can also seriously hurt your custody case. When a judge finds that you are using your son as a therapist and turning him against his mother, you may wonder if you have your best interest at heart. It is important not to tie things up during the divorce process but to talk to a trusted friend, family member, or psychologists such as a therapist or counselor.

When a marriage is falling apart, it's hard to avoid teasing your ex. However, regardless of what you think of her, it is best to work together to have a friendly relationship after the divorce.

After the divorce, you may never want to see your ex again, but that's not realistic when you have children. Although they are no longer husband and wife, they are co-parents and must communicate on some level while raising their children.

Please review some of the best practices for effective co-parenting and try implementing as many of them as possible. Of course, good co-parenting depends somewhat on your ex's cooperation, and that's out of your control.

If your ex is particularly nasty, consider using a co-parenting parallel parenting model to avoid conflict.

UNDERSTAND CHILD CUSTODY LAWS

Child custody can vary significantly from state to state, so first, you should familiarize yourself with the child custody laws in your jurisdiction.

Paying attention to the fine print is tedious, but it's the only way to know what you're dealing with before the custody hearing. Learning about the latest child custody laws can also help you create a list of questions to ask your divorce attorney as your court date approaches.

FOLLOW PROPER COURTROOM ETIQUETTE

Hoping to gain custody of your children, you must behave appropriately in court and follow proper protocols. Talk to your attorney about what to expect on the day of your hearing. It might be a good idea to role-play with your divorce attorney beforehand to ensure you understand the expectations before appearing in court.

You should also make sure to dress appropriately to make a positive impression. Typically, you'll want to wear something formal that conveys that you're organized and a responsible adult.

WORK TOGETHER TO KEEP THINGS FROM GETTING UGLY

One of the biggest problems with custody cases is that they can get ugly quickly. Parents often use this as an opportunity to vent frustrations related to their relationship with each other instead of focusing on their children.

If you want to protect your interests and children, you should do everything possible to make peace and be civilized. Try to separate yourself from your personal feelings about your ex and keep any unresolved issues between the two of you out of your custody case. Focus only on the issues that directly affect your child.

Regardless of where you stand, it is always best to settle out of court. You have more control over getting the best outcome for your child when your co-parenting is cooperative, not combative.

If you cannot agree, meditation services are available to work out the details necessary to go to court. Your lawyer can help you make these arrangements.

ALWAYS ADDRESS ISSUES THAT CAN WORK AGAINST YOU

When you face a custody battle, you can expect all aspects of your life to be scrutinized. Because of this, you need to understand what aspects of your life may not be working in your favor in court.

A lawyer can help you assess your circumstances and offer advice to give you the best chance of a favorable outcome. If potential issues are discovered, your attorney will advise you on minimizing the impact these things could have on your custody case.

Remember, too, that perception is everything. Maintain positive communication with the other parents, and don't tell them anything you wouldn't want a judge to see. The best thing you can do in the long term is to exercise your rights and fulfill your responsibilities as a parent. Even before a formal agreement is reached, take every opportunity to make a strong presence in your child's life and avoid making mistakes that could result in losing parental rights.

This is an ongoing issue, as you may need to amend your custody agreement in the future, so it's important to remember the above tips as you proceed. Understanding how to win a custody case means recognizing that there may not be a clear "winner."

The only proper way to see a custody battle outcome as a victory is when decisions are made in the best interests of the children involved.

CHAPTER 10
MY JOURNEY IN COURT

I was confident that I wouldn't have a good turnaround in my favor. My first appearance in court with my attorney was bittersweet. The type of allegations I was facing from the therapist be ing abusive and child molestation. I inappropriately touched my daughter the wrong way when I whacked her from voiding in her diapers. But before I had fought the allegations, I still had to show proof that I am the father. I was fortunate enough to get a DNA sample before everything transpired, and yes, I did it behind her back because I asked her before I did it and she was against it. The judge overruled her claims because nothing was consistent in her claims. There were no reports of me doing anything. The feelings I had during trial were past unbelievable. I took care of kids that weren't mine. I'm a first-time father at the age of 34. My daughter is my only child. I started my own business and I'm not running the streets. I didn't understand how someone could separate a child from the parent. I heard about these issues before, but it was never my problem, so I never paid attention to it. Then it hit me like a ton of bricks. How can you fight something like this? Is this beatable? What if you don't have the resources to fight this? Till this day my experience as a father has been a roller coaster. Being a father is already hard. Dealing with someone that refused to co-parent. When she got married it got even harder because she wanted to let her husband raise our daughter and pretend as if I didn't exist. My feelings in court were bottled up while my attorney fought for my character and it was brutal. However, I still had to go back to court because now I was fighting to have rights. Personally, it's embarrassing to go through this process because I'm not an argumentative person. I speak with reasoning. As an owner of a small business, I fixed situations all the time because I tried to see everyone's point of view.

Going to court for the second time for family court was drawn out for two years. I couldn't find the therapist's location of where she stayed, she moved twice in one year then when she got married. She convinced her husband I'm crazy I'm abusive I'm a child molester and I didn't want to be a father to my child because I stopped calling every day and I stopped text messaging her. It was mentally affecting me. I had to stop for health reasons and I fired my attorney because I felt like she wasn't fighting hard enough. I deeply regret firing my attorney prematurely. I attempt to hire another attorney that I found on the internet, but unfortunately they were based in California and wasn't able to give my case as much attention I felt it needed. I felt like I was only a number to them. I paid for their services but still had to file my own paperwork in the end. It was a complete waste of time and money. I learn that it is best to hire an attorney that you can physically go into their office to have direct access regarding your case. It was so difficult looking for an attorney while still trying to run my own business and keep my emotions intact. It was hard but I knew I needed to continue to take care of myself and work hard so that I can be a great provider for my daughter. I realized that I am no good to my daughter if my mental health wasn't intact.. How long can I keep this up? I had to take a break to get therapy and fight for her differently, so I did. When the time came to appear in court, the attorney I hired dropped my case because they claimed they're not getting paid enough therefore I ended up representing myself. My girlfriend at the time, which is now my wife, was my support system. I gave my wife all my text messages and all my receipts of me providing care for my daughter. My wife saw the nights I cried, she saw my mental health decreasing, she experienced the lack of trust I had in people, and she saw me neglecting myself and not eating properly. She not only helped me prepare for my case but helped me see who I was and that gave me the strength I needed to fight in court.

On the day of our last court appearance, I was extremely nervous. My bladder went into overdrive while waiting for the judge to call our case. Unfortunately, he waited to call our case last. Although my wife prepared every document I needed, nothing can prepare you for when you are face-to-face with a judge not knowing how he will respond to you. My mind went completely blank. It took me a minute to gain the confidence I needed to communicate and plead my case. Luckily, I didn't have to say much at all because she basically showed her true colors by not only trying to manipulate the judge, but she even lied, and the judge caught her. She was completely unprepared and even tried to bring our daughter up with her in her arms to manipulate the judge into sympathizing with her as if she is a hopeless single mother. The judge saw through all the games and lies. He ended up placing me on child support, which I requested but gave me joint custody of our daughter. I was elated to know that I can see my daughter without being controlled by her. She was pissed and upset because she wanted more money and control when I only wanted to be a father to our daughter. Most men don't volunteer to put themselves on child support where I'm from, but I wanted to support my daughter and I knew that this would also give me rights to her. So, all in all, there is a light at the end of the tunnel. You must keep fighting until the end for your child. It will be so worth it when your child is running to your arms. Don't give up! You will prevail.

CHAPTER 11
STRATEGIES

Child custody battles can be stressful! In today's lexicon, we can hardly say "custody" without uttering the word "battle" with it. Couples fighting for their children's custody have much more at stake than you think. Not only is there uncertainty about their future, but their children's quality of life also lies in their hands.

While undoubtedly every parent wants to give their children the best life possible, during a divorce, it's not up to the parents to decide what that is; only the court can decide for them. This is where the most amicable divorces can quickly turn ugly.

No matter the outcome of a custody case, the emotional turmoil takes a toll on a person's mental health. Since children don't understand divorces, courtrooms, or custody battles, navigating their emotions becomes tough. Judges are responsible for making decisions in their children's best interest.

During these difficult times, interacting with your children may become extremely difficult. Every interaction with your children will profoundly impact their mental and emotional well-being, so remain calm and collected. Now, you must be wondering how to work your way around doing this. Well, it's not as complicated as it looks. Every form of interaction with your child will be a form of communication.

The tone of your voice should matter. The look in your eyes and the kindness of your heart will also provide comfort. Your communication pattern will impact your child's emotional development and how they build relationships later in life.

WHAT ARE THE TYPES OF COMMUNICATION?

Communication can take two forms; it can be verbal and non-verbal.

Verbal Communication: It's the way we communicate with words and includes:

- Pitch and tone of voice
- The words you utter
- Dialect

Nonverbal Communication: Nonverbal communication can be both intentional and unintentional. It is made through body language. It includes:

- Facial expressions
- Eye contact
- Personal space
- Hand gestures
- Physical touch

Here are a few strategies that can enhance your communication.

1. Active Listening

Active listening helps children feel heard and understood. By using gestures like a smile and a nod of agreement, you can show that you care about what your child is saying and that you care. Putting yourself on the same level as your child as you talk to them can help them feel more secure and connected to you. Show that you listen carefully to what they say by asking questions such as "What?" "Because?" and "How?" This also helps your child improve their communication skills by teaching them how to tell a story and what details are included.

2. Reflective Listening

Acting like a mirror is a great way to show your child that you are paying attention and care about what they have to say. Repeat what they tell you using different words. For example, if your child says, "I don't play with Jacob anymore," you must reply, "Don't you play with your friend anymore?" This gives your child space to express their feelings without judgment. You will be surprised by how much they have to say.

3. Always Speak Clearly

Use language that your child understands and is age-appropriate. Be clear and specific. Also, don't use derogatory language. Kind language is a great way to set a positive example for your children. Remember that the conversation should make your little one feel respected and loved.

4. Avoid Bribes

The other party may offer bribes to close off the case. You might get tempted to accept it but don't fall victim to this trick. These temptations will always be there. Try to stick to your plan and avoid direct conversations with the partner you are fighting with. If your partner hits you up or wants you to talk to them over on call or over a meetup, inform your lawyer about everything and keep him confident.

5. Be Expressive

To help your child develop emotional intelligence, they must learn to name their feelings. When your child expresses their feelings verbally, listen to what they say with empathy and without judgment. Think about what life looks like through your eyes.

If your child expresses their feelings in non-verbal ways, for instance, by throwing a tantrum or laughing, help him or put his feelings into words. For instance, explain his feelings, whether they are happy, sad, relaxed, hurt, hungry, proud, or sleepy. Let your child tell you what he is feeling.

6. Use Noticing Statements

When you praise your child for specific actions, you help them feel good and let them know which behaviors you enjoy. Instead of saying, "Great Job!" try an "attention statement," more specifically, "I noticed that you put away all your toys after playing. Well done!"

7. Try Having Fun Together

As your children grow older, parenthood may seem more serious. That's why it's more important to have fun and light-hearted conversations together—a great way to strengthen your relationship!

Find ways to connect with your child by saying something positive about something important to them, listening to their interests, and fooling around together. Remember, laugh with your child, never at your child.

8. Focusing on Behavior

If you are upset about something about your child, make sure your criticism and comments are directed at their behavior and not at them as a person. For example, instead of saying, "I don't like it when you're messy," try saying, "I don't like it when you leave your clothes on the floor." Consider the example you set. Parents are introducing their children to the world. What your child sees in you is as important as what they hear you say.

These strategies will help you better understand your children in this challenging time. Similarly, there are many things you need to avoid while fighting for your child's custody battle. As an adult, you need to be quite wary of things.

9. Don't Ever Lie in Court

What you say in court and what you write on the court forms must be true. Lying in court during a custody battle will hurt your credibility.

The judge will see the truth in each parent's allegations

through custody assessments, witness statements, and other evidence presented at the hearing. Lying in court during a custody case can result in one parent losing custody or being responsible for paying the other parent's legal fees.

10. Don't Refuse to Participate in the Case

Since court cases are often stressful and expensive, you may be tempted to ignore the case altogether. However, you could lose time with your child if you don't attend a custody case.

If you do not respond to the other parent's petition, the court may enter a default judgment against you. This means the other parent gets everything they asked for without you contributing anything. Document requests and notifications to appear in court. Ignoring it may result in your case being dismissed. Be careful not to leave the city or country for an extended period, as these documents are usually sent to your last known address or place of work.

11. Don't Disrespect the Other Parent

In a custody case, the judge will determine whether a parent encourages a relationship between their ex and the child. Not respecting the other parent shows that you may not be capable of it. Insults directed at your ex via social media, calls, texts, and emails can affect judgment. You should also avoid commenting negatively about your ex in front of others. What you say could come to light in court through the testimony of a witness.

12. Never Withhold Your Child

Hiding your child from the other parent is unique compared to other things you shouldn't do during a custody battle because it comes with a caveat: keeping the child away from the other parent may be your only option when the parent presents a clear danger.

If there is no security risk, denying the other parent access to the child will negatively affect you. The courts prefer to involve both parents in the child's life and want to see that you can foster a positive relationship between your child and your ex.

13. Keep Your Child Away from the Case

Your child may be the subject of the custody battle but putting them in the middle will cause you unnecessary stress. Spare them the case details and focus on maintaining the routines the child is used to and spending quality time together. Distractions from what's happening at home, like extracurricular activities, are especially helpful in facilitating some sense of normalcy.

14. Avoid Bringing New Partners into Your Life

Bringing a new partner into your child's life is an often-overlooked example of what not to do during a custody battle. Your child will be in a weak state during this time. A new partner could cause confusion and anger if your child assumes they are trying to replace their other parent.

Do not bring a new partner into the case if you have a new partner. Judges often frown on parents taking their partners to court because their presence could be distracting. Outside of court, you should minimize interactions between your partner and your ex. Any confrontation that occurs could help your ex's case.

15. Don't Push for a Trial without Compromising

The trial should be the last resort after all other attempts at resolution have failed. Maintain ownership of parenting decisions and start your co-parenting relationship by negotiating an agreement with the other parent. Suppose you're having trouble resolving the disagreement between the two of you. Try an alternative dispute resolution method.

16. Don't Show Up to Court Unprepared

Preparation is critical in a custody battle. You must come to court prepared with a proposed parenting plan and provide solid evidence to support your claims. If you have a lawyer, they will help you prepare.

If you are representing yourself, check your state's child custody laws and rules of evidence to avoid presenting evidence that the court cannot consider. For instance, recording a telephone conversation without the other person's permission is illegal in some states. Illegally obtained recordings damage your credibility and cannot be used in court.

17. Try Not to Disregard Court Orders

Preliminary orders are often part of divorce and custody cases. These orders will remain in effect until the court issues final orders.

If you have court orders for child support or parental leave, follow them. Failure to do so shows a lack of respect for the court and that you may be unable to comply with the final custody order.

Also, don't get into the habit of delaying time with your children. Be on time for pickup and drop off as scheduled to show the court that you can comply with orders. Only deviate from the arrangement in an absolute emergency and inform the other parent when there is time.

You will notice a significant change in your kids and your life when you demonstrate these attributes in your behavior and attitudes. In my case, handling my child wasn't that big of a deal because my daughter was still an infant.

She wasn't at the age where she could understand emotions or comprehend what was happening in her life. Otherwise, things would have been more challenging for me. However, I do understand that infant trauma is a real thing too. Children only a few months old can feel the negative impact of harsh events in their lives.

Many believe breaking marriages or relationships while their kids are young might not cause adverse effects; however, that is not the case. An infant can feel extreme emotions just as a toddler. Keeping this in mind, I did extensive research on infant-based trauma.

It turns out that trauma can seriously disrupt essential aspects of your child's development. This can occur before the age of three years. These may include relationships and bonding with parents and the impact of their language, mobility, and physical and social skills. However, their capacity to navigate their emotions might deteriorate as they grow up. These infants might fall victim to ADHD with complex anxiety issues and slowed cognitive abilities over time.

Babies and toddlers are extremely helpless and depend on their families and parents to provide them with safety and security. Through loving and reassuring interactions, their need for emotional nurturing can help them cope continuously and consistently. This is how babies and toddlers develop themselves and grow.

Children can be very sensitive to:

- Problems that affect their parents, caregivers, or siblings can trigger fear, sadness, and depression in them.
- Separation from their parents, primary caregivers, or absence due to injury can also cause trauma. This can cause damage at an alarming rate: distress from the separation combined with the insecurity of having to manage without caregivers. Both can slowly recover and elevate the effect of trauma.
- Also, too much noise in a household can adversely affect the brain, allowing them to become sensitive to noise.
- Disruptions to developing a bond or close relationship with their parents can lack parental understanding.
- Trauma can sometimes get in the way, making forming this bond difficult.

If any of this is happening, it's essential to prioritize the effect on the baby. If the family or primary carer is affected, the baby will probably also be affected.

CHAPTER 12
FIND YOUR SILVER LINING

"Even sorrow has its silver lining, as the emotion that pours forth reminds us of our capacity to love and to be loved."

—Rob Kozak, *Finding Fatherhood*

After reading this quote, you might think, *how can sorrowful moments help us teach life lessons?* But let me tell you one thing, in our adversities, the true meaning of our lives is hidden. These dark clouds pour bursting over our heads for a reason. Now, you see, this is how life works. We aren't put in these troublesome times without any reason. It's always God's plan; he is the one who wants us to put in more effort in testing out our strengths. He wants us to become stronger whenever we face any despair.

I never wished to be in the position I am in today, but there, I feel helpless. Sometimes, I had epiphanies that led me to believe I was evolving. I had come a long way from a person who was gullible in the beginning. I have always struggled with keeping boundaries, but gradually, I became good at maintaining and creating new ones daily. It's funny how nobody tells you about these huge scary roads you will be taking in your life; nobody prepares you for the storms that will pass in your life. You need to experience one to learn the hard life lessons they tend to throw at you.

I hope these downpours come with disclaimers or some warning that can help us avoid the chaos in no time. Unfortunately, that's not how life works; we must step on each stone in our path. Every stone is beautifully laid to teach us a lesson.

I am sure most of you are familiar with the words "silver lining."

For those who aren't buckled up, I will elaborate on it right here. A silver lining is a ray of hope you seek during a difficult time. Major life events such as a relative's death, surviving a car crash, or in my case, a child custody battle can destroy a critical relationship. A person can become severely depressed or painfully isolated during this period. They might fail to open up to their loved ones or life.

Silver linings don't just magically appear out of nowhere; a person always looks for them. It's up to a person and his courage to look at the brighter things in life. Well, I know you must all think I may have gone nuts with this piece of advice I am jotting down but trust me, I am writing it with a great personalized experience. If I didn't fight the custody battle for my child, I wouldn't be writing these scriptures down on a bright sunny Tuesday afternoon.

Don't let these traumatic experiences pull you down; sometimes, these tragic events bring about unexpected positive experiences.

1. You Learn to Become More Compassionate

Experiencing suffering for yourself can make you more compassionate toward others going through the same. When people witness the difficulties of others, they often, for reasons, try to blame the victim for their situation (e.g., "He has financial problems because he doesn't work hard enough," or "She is ill because she works too much and doesn't take care of herself") thereby reducing their sense of vulnerability. But when you have suffered deeply, you are more likely to realize that everyone is vulnerable and that bad things happen to good people all the time. Another person's suffering is no longer a threat but can be a source of connection and kinship.

2. You Discover Hidden Strengths

In the early stages of an adverse life event, you might think, "There's no way I'm going to get through this." But somehow, day after day, you manage to put one foot in front of the other; despite the pain you may be feeling, you always make it through.

One of the ways difficulties show you is with the true strength you never knew you had until you tested it. Research on affective prognosis supports this idea, suggesting that we overestimate how devastating and adverse life events will make us and how long the pain will last; in other words, we are more resilient than we think.

3. You Learn Who Your True Friends Are

During difficult times, certain relationships are likely to deepen while others fade. Finding out that some people are friends in the good times and disappear when you need them can be extremely painful. However, it's also an opportunity to develop a new appreciation for the people who stay and direct your energy toward those relationships' focus. Research suggests that sometimes, even with the weakest of social ties, people you weren't close with, to begin with, the occasion can prove very supportive in stressful situations.

4. You Get More Clarity in Life

Sometimes a crisis can cause you to reevaluate your life in meaningful ways. It can force you to question whether you're doing what makes you happy and spending time the way you want. As jarring as these assessments are, for one reason or another, they can push you to make positive changes that didn't previously seem like realistic possibilities: fear of failure, worry about what other people would think, or just plain inertia about the status quo. But those factors don't carry as much weight when the reality that life is fragile and unpredictable takes hold.

After following the above tips, you can always find tranquility among angst. Once you understand the dynamics of your complications and journey, things will get easier for you, so don't get disheartened. I know it's hard to look at the bright side when your entire world has crashed, but this is your only hope.

I'll explain this concept by telling you a short story I read in a book long ago. So, once upon a time, there was a girl named Lily in a small village surrounded by mountains. Lily was known for being cheerful and optimistic but received bad news one day. Her father, the family's sole breadwinner, had lost his job, and they struggled to make ends meet.

At first, Lily was devastated. She knew that her family's financial situation would be difficult, and she couldn't afford the things she used to do. But as the days passed, Lily started to look for a silver lining in her situation. Known for her cheerful and optimistic nature, she began to help her mother with household chores and cared for her younger siblings. She also started to explore her village's mountains and surroundings, looking for herbs and berries that could be sold at the local market.

One day, while in the woods, she stumbled upon an abandoned cabin. The cabin was small and rustic but had a beautiful garden and a small stream nearby. Lily realized that the cabin could be her family's income source.

She cleaned the cabin and rented it to tourists who wanted to experience mountain life. As the months passed, Lily's cabin became very popular, and she earned enough money to support her family. She also made new friends and learned a lot about the mountains and the animals that lived there.

Lily realized that sometimes bad things happen to us to make us stronger and more resourceful. She knew that she could handle any challenge that came her way and that she could always find a way to turn things around.

From that day on, Lily lived her life with a positive attitude. Failing to be hopeful during hard times can have several drawbacks, including:

1. Prolonged Negative Emotions

If you cannot find anything positive in difficult situations, you may feel overwhelmed by negative emotions, such as sadness, anger, or despair. These emotions can affect your mental health, well-being, relationships, and ability to function effectively.

2. Missed Opportunities

Not finding a silver lining can also mean missing opportunities to learn and grow from difficult experiences. Adversity can be an influential teacher, and valuable lessons or insights may be gained from the most challenging situations.

3. Limited Perspective

Focusing only on the negative aspects of hard times can limit your perspective and prevent you from seeing the bigger picture. You can see the situation from different angles and better understand what is happening by finding a silver lining.

Motivating yourself during hardships can be a challenging task, but it is essential for ensuring that you remain engaged and productive.

To cope with the difficult times, I would use that energy to motivate others. Here are some tips I used to help motivate others that in turn helped me feel better about what I was going through:

- **Listen and Empathize:** One of the most important things you can do is to listen to them and show empathy. People in hardship feel like no one understands what they're going through, so taking the time to listen and show understanding can be a great motivator.
- **Provide Support:** Whether emotional or practical, make sure you're there for them. Offer to help them with their daily tasks or be a shoulder to lean on when needed.
- **Encourage Them to Take Action:** It's essential to encourage people in hardships to take action and not give up. Help them identify small steps they can take toward their goals and encourage them to take action.
- **Celebrate Their Successes:** Celebrate every small victory along the way. Acknowledge their progress and encourage them to keep going.
- **Provide Inspiration:** Share stories of people who have overcome similar hardships and succeeded. Show them that it is possible to overcome tough times and become stronger.
- **Be Positive:** Your attitude can significantly impact

those around you. Stay optimistic and help them see the light at the end of the tunnel.

- **Help Them Find Meaning:** Encourage them to find meaning in their hardships. Help them see that there is a lesson to be learned and that they can grow from this experience.

Without faith, hope, and yearning, your life will have no meaning. I hope these tips shape your future for the better. Try relying on God by trusting his plans; you will get what you desire sooner or later.

CHAPTER 13
NEVER GIVE UP

"Could she be happy outside my daily, direct control?
The answer was yes. It was a blow to my ego, but it was
true. The epiphany lifted a great weight off my shoulders.
Even though I could not understand the grand scheme of
things, I could see what was truly important when I applied
a simple filter—my child's well-being—to the situation."
—Ranjani Rao, *Rewriting My Happily Ever After —*
A Memoir of Divorce and Discovery

This quote touched my heart, so I incorporated it into this in-credible book I am writing. My journey has been full of ups and downs. It's not like I have only met the negative side of it. There have been times when I have felt rejuvenated when I have met with the darker side of situations and have learned to evolve. There was a time when I would get multiple mental breakdowns daily when I had lost complete control of my life.

There have been times when I have felt my confidence crumble to the ground where I had no energy to pick up the pieces. Also, I had no one beside me during those times of dismay. The evenings were the worst; my heart would become heavy. As the sky grad-ually darkened, so would my mind, heart, and soul. I would pause momentarily; you might have seen this happening when people zone out of conversations.

In those moments, I would realize the harsh reality of life. Those evenings made and broke me; I will never forget them. I want my audience to know that their journey doesn't end here. They still have a long way to go, a long wide road ready to take you on new endeavors, adventures, and destinations. God writes this path for you. You might need to take control of your life, but there will always be something you cannot fully overcome. This is where trust in that superior power comes in. It would be best if you mustered up the courage to leave a few things to him and entirely put faith in his plan.

Building yourself with this perception will lift you in unimaginable ways. You will explore yourself in ways you never have. You'll discover strengths that you never thought existed in you. Life will take a new turn from them, and you will see it change gradually. I encourage my audience to develop a healthy relationship with superior power. When people become close to God, they have nothing to lose. They would understand that all struggles thrown their way are for their growth.

Another approach for battling a custody battle is by keeping yourself knowledgeable about the various impacts it can have on both the parent's and children's mental health. I would suggest that my audience conducts in-depth research on how to combat several psychological challenges through these difficult times. Most parents know that divorce and child custody battles can be brutal. However, many parents underestimate the impact their behavior toward the other parent (good and bad) and their willingness to co-parent can have on their children. If you want to mitigate the psychological impact of custody battles on your child, be courteous to the other parent, seek advice, think long-term, and be flexible if things change.

I want to present a few research findings that demonstrate how harmful health consequences might affect children's developing minds.

Children and adolescents who experience parental separation and divorce are more likely to experience adjustment problems, child custody issues, poorer academic performance, misbehavior, substance addiction, and depression, according to research published in the American Sociological Review.

When parents do not get along, these issues are made worse. The American Psychological Association (APA) states that

"Parental conflict often has a profound emotional impact on children caught in the middle, leading to increased dropout rates, behavioral problems, and health problems."[1]

I experience this again and again. Children are like sponges, and when their parents constantly fight and talk negatively about each other, that negative energy and fear seep into them.

For example, I recently saw a parent who was very angry with the other parent and spoke negatively about that other parent in front of the child. You could see the fear on the poor boy's face.

This child has been receiving negative influence from the other parent for some time, so, unsurprisingly, the child is scared and afraid to go to the other parent's house. That parent was someone the child loved and had a close relationship with before the divorce and custody battle.

They now feel that going to the other parent's house is unsafe and that something terrible will happen when they get there. All because of the unnecessary argument, bitterness, and tension between the two parents.

There could be scenarios where your children can suffer massively, and the inability to bring their minds to ease can also take a toll on you. Parents do not feel good watching their children go through sleepless nights and torment. This situation makes things worse. Resorting to therapy might be a good solution. Many have witnessed healthy improvements in their life after taking multiple therapy sessions, but unfortunately, things were a bit different in my case.

All my life, I have heard that therapy helps people going through tough times come to terms with their current situation and overcome the devastating aftereffects. People suffering from depression have also been seen enjoying a fulfilling life after undergoing therapy. But all I can say is it's different for different people. What one might feel after a few sessions may not be the same for another person.

---

[1] Justin Sisemore, *How to Mitigate the Psychological Effects of Child Custody Battles.* The American Sociological Review, 2022.

Our paths are different; we all have other stories to tell. Likewise, our struggles are dissimilar as well. I am not sure about becoming less depressed after seeking therapy, but there is one thing I can take forward with me: resilience.

At its core, resilience means adapting and recovering when something difficult happens. It is the ability to bounce back after trauma or a painful experience.

Our level of resilience will change and evolve throughout our lives, and at times we will find that we are not coping as well as others. In another sense, strength is just one of the many psychological tools we use to help us feel normal again.

As we all know, when we are in a weakened position where we feel things are going wrong, it can be tough to find our balance, swim against the tide, or recover and regain stability, getting worse. Resilience is essential for several reasons. It allows us to develop protective mechanisms against experiences that might be overwhelming, helps us maintain balance in our lives during difficult or stressful times, and can also protect us from creating some mental health difficulties and problems.

The benefits of resilience that you should ponder upon:

- Improving learning and academic performance.
- Minors are absent from work or study due to illness.
- Reducing risky behaviors such as excessive drinking, smoking, or drug use.
- Increased participation in community or family activities.
- Lower mortality rate and better physical health.

ITS MEANING IN PSYCHOLOGY

Resilient people often do more than recover. After a significant event, such as the death of a loved one or an unexpectedly wrong medical diagnosis, even the most resilient person is unlikely to bounce back or at least stay the same.

In contrast, psychology recognizes that resilient people going through significant life events do not always bounce back quickly, they often find a new way.

- **A New or Revised Self-Image**

Resilient people become aware of incredible abilities as they face each new challenge.

- **Enriched and Clarified Relationships**

In difficult times, they recognize friends who stay and offer support and those who no longer call back or are toxic or exhausting and prioritize positive relationships.

- **Changed Priorities**

A fresh and possibly more focused perspective can eliminate the unimportant and clarify and motivate essential values, life goals, and priorities. Moreover, a renewed purpose can also derive from a person who is already resilient in their actions.

SIGNS OF RESILIENCE IN LIFE

- **Reframing**

Looking at a problem or situation from a different and more helpful perspective can help the person deal with it.

- **Harnessing the Power of Positive Emotion**

Such feelings expand our thinking and allow us to develop alternative strategies to solve problems more creatively. They can also strengthen our sense of belonging, helping us connect with supportive people and groups and increasing our understanding of accomplishment and ideas of purposeful living.

- **Participate in Physical Activities**

Being more active can help manage and reduce the effects of stress while improving confidence and self-esteem.

- **Ongoing Active Engagement in Trusted Social Networks**

Social support from trusted friends, coworkers, and family members can make us feel less isolated and help us gain a better perspective on what is happening.

- **Identifying and Utilizing Your Strength**

Using our strengths, we can feel more authentic and increase our sense of purpose and control when facing new challenges or overcoming adversity.

- **Optimistic Approach to Life**

Looking to the future with optimism can help us recognize that setbacks are often temporary and surmountable and help us be more optimistic about the future.

After seeking therapy, I found a profound change in my life. A kind of revolution that was persistent. There is no other way of going about it. So, whenever the nights get longer for me and the silence grows dark, I sit alone like a lone wolf trying to connect the dots. Trying to find meaning or a purpose in the life I have lived. To my surprise, till now, I haven't been able to find any answers, but I hope the people reading my book do so.

So, in this last concluding chapter, I wish to encourage all my readers, especially the ones on this single-parenting journey, to take time for themselves and take things slow. You can have it figured out all at once. Try to be patient as much as possible with yourself and seek therapy if you wish. Put your faith in the Almighty and let it all go.

ACKNOWLEDGMENTS

I would like to thank my mother and father, Joann, and James Harris, my lovely and beautiful wife, Myesha, my aunt Thomasina Hollis, the Ford family out of Miami, and all my friends and colleagues that have supported me throughout my journey.

ABOUT THE AUTHOR

Asaph Brown is a hardworking businessman that started his own trucking company when he barely had a place to lay his head. He sacrificed his own vital needs to build his company because he knew he needed to provide for his daughter. He is a native of Miami Gardens, Florida. He is a father, son, brother, friend, nephew, and cousin to a beautiful family. He's always strived for excellence but also remains humble in all his works. He's a man of few words but will give you the shirt off his back. Asaph wears many hats. He started his career in modeling during his teen years which eventually led him to the performing arts where he became an actor. He recently completed a short film in which he played one of the leading roles. Asaph has always had a passion for writing and is excited to finally publish his first book. He feels it will help a lot of people who can relate with his struggle to be a part of his child's life.

Printed in the USA
CPSIA information can be obtained
at www.ICGtesting.com
LVHW010352020624
781922LV00004B/546

9 781665 307888